T0266580

WHO WOULD WIN?

JAGUAR

VS.

SKUNK

BY
JERRY PALLOTTA

ILLUSTRATED BY
ROB BOLSTER

Scholastic Inc.

*The publisher would like to thank the following for their
kind permission to use their photographs in this book:
Photos ©: 1 center right: Isselee/Dreamstime; 4: anankkml/Thinkstock;
5: Isselee/Dreamstime; 6 bottom: André Baertschi/wildtropix.com;
16 bottom: Fabiofersa/Dreamstime; 20 top: krinkog/Fotolia;
21 bottom: Courtesy Skunk Works® Lockheed Martin Corporation;
24 center: Julesuyttenbroeck/Dreamstime; 29 top: Panoramic Images/Getty Images.*

Thank you to Barbara Burns and all my pals at Norfolk Academy.
—J.P.
Dedicated to all who make their living on the ocean.
—R.B.

hat would happen if a skunk and a jaguar came nose to
se? If they had a fight, who do you think would win?

MEET THE JAGUAR

The jaguar is a mammal in the cat family. It is the third largest cat on Earth. The jaguar is a skilled hunter and excellent swimmer. Its scientific name is *Panthera onca*

DEFINITION
A mammal is a warm-blooded animal that often has hair or fur.

BIG FACT
The Siberian tiger is the largest of all cats.

SECOND FACT
The lion is the second-largest cat.

MEET THE SKUNK

e skunk is a mammal in the Mephitidae family. A
iped skunk's scientific name is *Mephitis mephitis*,
ich means "bad smell." Skunks have black-and-white
.

FACT
*The word "skunk" comes
from the Algonquin Indian
language.*

he skunk is not known for its scary teeth or sharp claws.
is famous because it can make a stink!

CLIMB

Jaguars can climb trees. They often drag their freshly killed prey up into the branches of a tree.

SWIM

Most cats do not like to go in the water, but the jaguar is an excellent swimmer. Watch out, crocodiles! Watch out, turtles!

HIDE

The skunk is good at hiding. It is rarely seen during daylight. Where is the skunk?

NOISY FACT
If you hear an animal on your roof, it's probably a raccoon or a squirrel, not a skunk.

QUESTION
Have you ever smelled a skunk in your neighborhood?

Under the house? In the trash can? Over there by the bushes?

**jaguar:
rosettes**

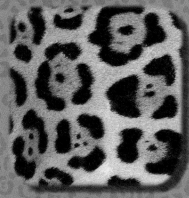

FUR FACT

*Most black panthers
are jaguars or leopards
without spots.*

**leopard:
c-shaped spots**

**cheetah:
polka dots**

**tiger:
stripes**

**lion:
plain**

BABY FACT

*A baby lion has white
spots, which it usually
outgrows.*

KNOW YOUR STRIPES

zorilla

hog-nosed skunk

spotted skunk

hooded skunk

FURRY FACT
Baby skunks are born with stripes.

striped skunk

This is a stinky page! In this book we will feature the striped skunk.

x

The jaguar lives in much of Central America and South America.

NORTH AMERICA

PACIFIC OCEAN

ATLANTIC OCEAN

CENTRAL AMERICA

SOUTH AMERICA

jaguar territory

FACT
Jaguars do not live in Africa.

Many jaguars live in rain forests. They also hunt on grassland and savannas.

WORLD

Skunks are found on every continent except Antarctica and Australia.

RCTIC OCEAN

EUROPE

ASIA

PACIFIC
OCEAN

FRICA

INDIAN
OCEAN

skunk
territory

AUSTRALIA

SOUTHERN OCEAN

ANTARCTICA

11

CREPUSCULAR

The jaguar sometimes is a crepuscular hunter.

DEFINITION

"Crepuscular" means an animal hunts at dawn and at dusk.

AUTO FACT

There is a famous sports car called the Jaguar.

Dawn is when the sun first rises. Dusk is when the sun

TIME-OF-DAY FACTS

Dawn is also called daybreak. Dusk is also called twilight.

NOCTURNAL

The skunk is a nocturnal hunter. It comes out at night.

"Hey, Rob, maybe we should write a nocturnal alphabet book." —Jerry

The **NOCTURNAL** Alphabet Book

BY
JERRY PALLOTTA
ILLUSTRATED BY
ROB BOLSTER
SCHOLASTIC

DINNER

Zoologists studied jaguars and discovered that they eat dozens of different types of animals.

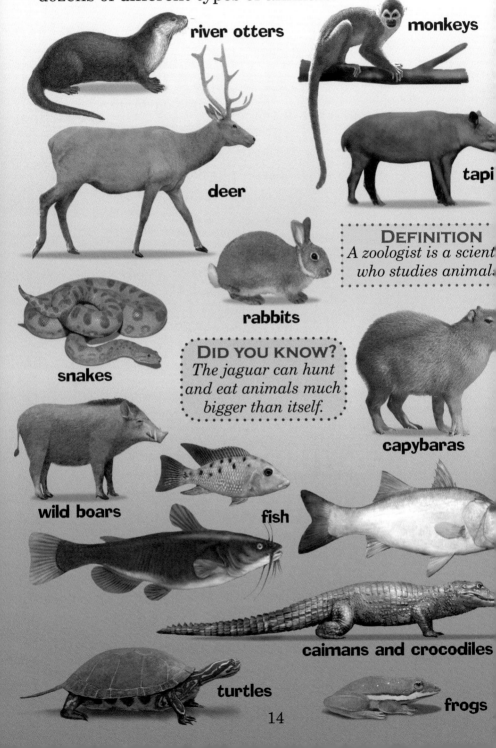

river otters

monkeys

deer

tapi

rabbits

DEFINITION
*A zoologist is a scient
who studies animal.*

snakes

DID YOU KNOW?
*The jaguar can hunt
and eat animals much
bigger than itself.*

capybaras

wild boars

fish

caimans and crocodiles

turtles

frogs

14

SUPPER

Skunks are omnivores. They eat plants and animals. A skunk would gladly eat spaghetti or a cheeseburger, too.

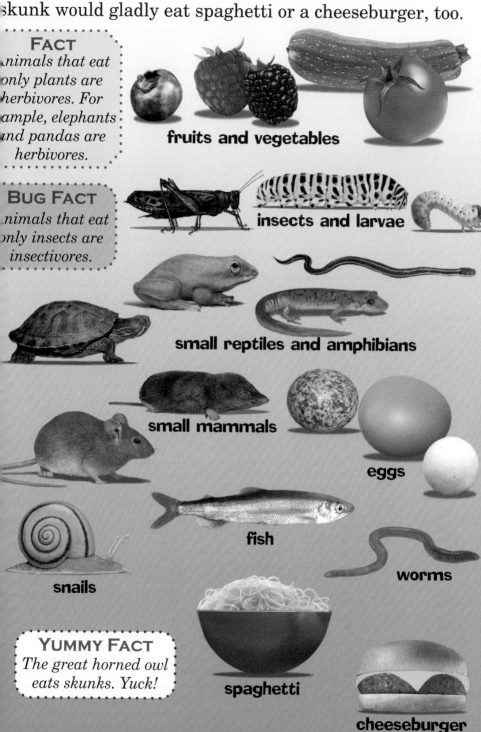

fruits and vegetables

insects and larvae

small reptiles and amphibians

small mammals

eggs

fish

worms

snails

spaghetti

cheeseburger

WARNING BEWARE THE JAGUAR

The jaguar is a magnificent creature. If there were an anir Olympics, the jaguar might win the gold medal for huntin

However, the jaguar is not a gentle animal. It stalks and ambushes its prey. Its jaws are so strong it can bite turtle shells, pierce skulls, and crush necks.

TAIL FACT

The jaguar has the shortest tail of all the big cats; the snow leopard has the longest tail.

WARNING BEWARE THE SKUNK

One day, a skunk sprayed the underside of a car. The car smelled so bad the family couldn't drive it for a week. Stinky!

A skunk was near a home's outdoor air-conditioning unit. The skunk got startled and sprayed. The smell went through the central air vents in the house, and the people couldn't live there for a month. It wasn't funny!

A girl got sprayed by a skunk on her way to school. The principal sent her home. To get the skunk smell off, she had to take a bath in tomato juice. Her parents had to throw her clothes away.

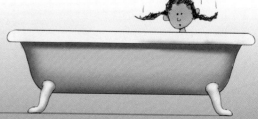

17

HEAR

How might you know a jaguar is in the area? You would hear it! The jaguar is the only cat in the Western Hemisphere that roars.

> **MEOW FACT**
> *House cats meow.*
> *Lions, tigers, leopards,*
> *and jaguars roar!*

SMELL

How would you know a skunk is in the area? You might smell it! Yuck! The skunk's smell comes from glands near its tail. The skunk lifts its tail and shoots its stinky mist.

FACT

Skunks are less likely to spray if they can't see what they are spraying. If a pest-removal worker catches a skunk in a cage, he might cover the cage with a blanket so the skunk won't spray.

ALONE

The jaguar is a solitary cat. It is perfectly happy living alone.

DEFINITION
"Solitary" and "solo" both mean "alone."

This might be what it would look like if jaguars hunted in a pack. Yikes!

SOLO FACT
The tiger is a solitary hunter.

PACK FACT
The lion is a pack hunter.

COOL SMELLY FACTS

The name "Chicago" is from the Ojibwa Indian language for "skunk land."

CHICAGO SKYLINE

Skunk Works® was the secret name of the Lockheed Martin aircraft factory in Palmdale, California, which built the top secret U-2 spy plane, the SR-71 Blackbird, the F-117 Nighthawk stealth fighter, and the F-22 Raptor.

TEETH

The jaguar has teeth that are perfect for catching and eating meat.

HEIGHT AND WEIGHT

26"-30" HIGH AT SHOULDER

36 INCHES

24

12

0

WEIGHT
120–210 pounds

LITTLE JAW

The skunk has small teeth, but they do the job!

DID YOU KNOW?
A skunk's smell is made up of seven chemicals.

DID YOU KNOW?
Some skunks do handstands so they appear larger.

LENGTH AND WEIGHT

INCHES

0   12   24   36

22"-31" LONG

WEIGHT
4–12 pounds

MORE WEAPONS

The jaguar has other weapons besides its huge teeth an strong jaws.

SHARP CLAWS

CAMOUFLAGE

SPEED/QUICKNESS

Wow! A jaguar can run fifty miles per hour. That is really moving!

ONE WEAPON

Maybe all you need is one secret weapon. The skunk's ability to create a terrible smell has kept it safe for millions of years.

DID YOU KNOW?
The skunk can shoot its spray up to six times in a row before it runs out.

FACT
Skunk spray is highly flammable.

STINK

Skunks aren't fast. But they are experts in chemical warfare.

The jaguar sneaks up on a napping crocodile and crush
its neck with one giant bite!

As the jaguar was eating the crocodile, the skunk found a
tasty dragonfly.

I wish I was a human. I'd have a pepperoni pizza, a cheeseburger, and fries.

As the jaguar was eating a nutria, the skunk was munching on a delicious frog.

DEFINITION
A *nutria* is a kind of water rat.

The jaguar ambushes a capybara, the largest rodent on Earth. It hauls the big rodent up its tree to save for a dinner later.

DEFINITION
An ambush is a surprise attack.

A big green anaconda for lunch also is no problem. The jaguar's jaws are strong! Sorry, snake!

he jaguar catches a giant pacu with its pointy teeth. Yum!
; will have fish for dinner tonight.

s the jaguar was eating the giant pacu, the skunk
newed and swallowed a turtle egg.

FACT
*A skunk was seen
chasing a cougar away.*

The jaguar's jaw is so strong it can pierce a tough turtle shell. The jaguar will eat the turtle.

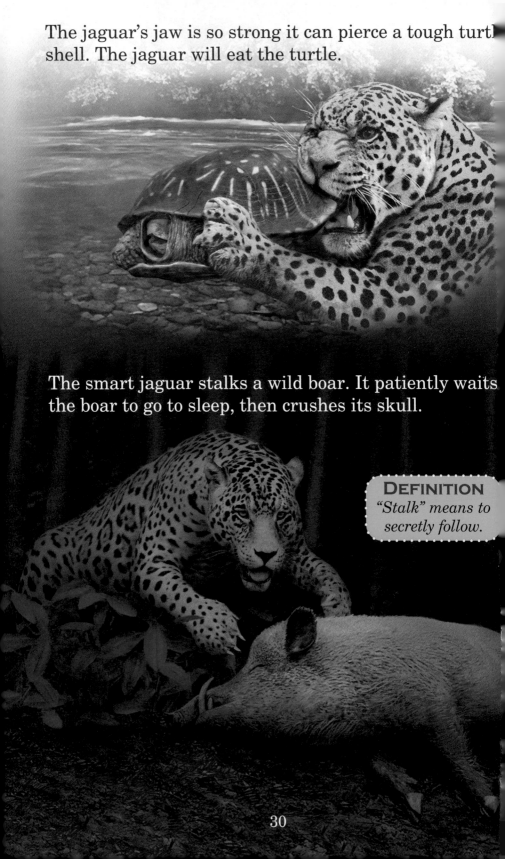

The smart jaguar stalks a wild boar. It patiently waits the boar to go to sleep, then crushes its skull.

DEFINITION
"Stalk" means to secretly follow.

The hungry jaguar is walking in the rain forest. It is
ooking for another meal.

he jaguar sees the skunk. The jaguar could easily rip
ie skunk to shreds. This may be no contest.

The jaguar can't stand the smell. It runs away as fast as possible. Congratulations to the skunk. The ferocious jaguar quit the battle. STINK WINS!

WHO HAS THE ADVANTAGE? CHECKLIST

JAGUAR		SKUNK
☐	Size	☐
☐	Teeth	☐
☐	Stink	☐
☐	Claws	☐
☐	Speed	☐
☐	Weight	☐

Author's note: Maybe you can write your own Who Would Win? book. Who do you think a jaguar should fight?